ART IN THE RENAISSANCE

BY ERIC CHRISTOPHER MEYER

TABLE OF CONTENTS

INTRODUCTION

Leonardo da Vinci. Michelangelo. Raphael. Do these names sound familiar? They are famous artists. They lived and worked in a period of time called the Renaissance (REN-uh-zahns). The Renaissance lasted from the mid-1300s through the 1600s. During these years, great changes happened in art and science. These changes began in Italy. The changes slowly spread across Europe.

The term *renaissance* comes from the French word *renaître*. This means "to be born again." Renaissance scholars had a renewed interest in learning. They studied the art, books, and buildings of ancient Greece and Rome.

▲ Renaissance artists were inspired by the sculptures of ancient Greece and Rome. These sculptures are from the Acropolis in Athens, Greece.

◀ The period known as the Renaissance began in Italy in the 1300s and then spread throughout Europe.

Many of these scholars were **humanists**. Humanists focused on people. They thought that learning could improve people's lives.

Before the Renaissance, most works of art were religious. Artists often painted people or stories from the Bible. Most scholars studied religious ideas. But humanists wanted to study more than religion. Humanists studied poetry, philosophy, music, drama, and art.

The change in thinking brought about great changes in art. Artists began creating art about nonreligious subjects, too. They painted portraits of people and places.

Renaissance artists created some of the world's greatest art. Learn about these masterpieces in art, sculpture, and **architecture**. Imagine the life and times of the great artists as you read.

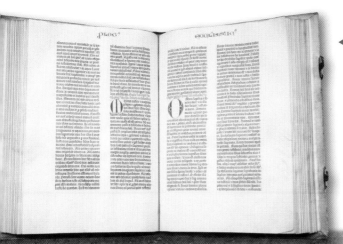

◀ Around 1450, Johannes Gutenberg perfected the printing press. The printing press allowed more people to have books.

RENAISSANCE PAINTING

During the Renaissance, artists often traveled. They visited well-known master artists. Some of these older artists held school-like workshops. Young artists came to study and practice painting and sculpting.

Other artists journeyed to the courts of ruling families. These **patrons** supported them. Patrons sometimes paid for an artist's food and lodging. Other times, they hired artists to create art. Patrons held parties and other social events. An artist with a powerful patron often found fame.

▲ This painting, *The Virgin and Child with Saint*, by da Vinci, shows the artist's mastery of perspective.

Perspective

The use of **perspective** (puhr-SPEHK-tihv) helped to define Renaissance painting. Perspective made paintings look more realistic.

Pre-Renaissance paintings had few background details. Renaissance artists, however, began to paint differently. Human figures were presented in front of landscapes. These landscapes shrunk in size as they disappeared into the distance.

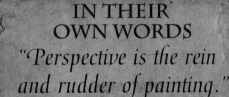

IN THEIR
OWN WORDS
"Perspective is the rein and rudder of painting."
—Leonardo da Vinci

◀ Renaissance artists began to use linear perspective in their art. Notice how the trees are smaller than the people in the front of the picture.

Leonardo da Vinci

Renaissance painters applied their knowledge of human anatomy to their work. Anatomy is the study of the human body. Painters began showing the human body at its strongest. Leonardo da Vinci was a master at showing the human form.

Da Vinci was born in 1452 near Florence, Italy. As a child, he drew detailed pictures of the world around him. He decided to be an artist. He moved to Florence to become an apprentice (uh-PREN-tis). An apprentice is someone who learns a craft or trade by working with a skilled person. His teacher was painter and sculptor Andrea del Verrocchio.

By 1472, da Vinci was accepted into the honored Florence painters' guild. A guild is a group of people in the same trade. A guild protects the interests of its members. Being in the guild allowed da Vinci to accept **commissions**. A commission is money for work done. Important, well-paying jobs went only to guild members.

◄ Leonardo da Vinci drew this self-portrait when he was about sixty years old. It is the only picture of the artist that exists today.

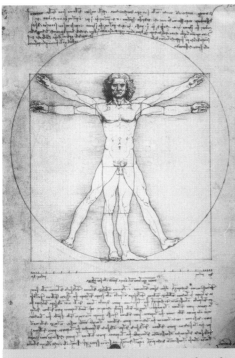

▲ Leonardo da Vinci's notebooks have given us a firsthand look into the creative mind of the artist.

In 1482, da Vinci went to Milan to work. He stayed for sixteen years. While there, he painted, sculpted, and designed. He also studied the human body. To do this, he performed dissections. A dissection is the careful cutting apart of a dead body to study it. He sketched and wrote about his ideas in notebooks.

HISTORICAL PERSPECTIVE

Leonardo da Vinci was a painter, sculptor, architect, engineer, musician, and scientist. He designed a helicopter and experimented with photography.

Leonardo da Vinci inspired the term "Renaissance Man." Today, this term describes someone who has mastered many subjects.

In 1500, Leonardo da Vinci returned to Florence. He needed money, so the artist accepted a commission in 1503. It led to the most famous portrait in history.

Mystery surrounds the *Mona Lisa*. Many believe she was the wife of a merchant from Florence. The name *Mona Lisa* is short for *Madonna Lisa* or "my lady Lisa."

In the original painting, da Vinci placed his subject on a balcony. She was surrounded by a landscape. After da Vinci's death, someone made the painting smaller. They cut out the columns of the balcony. No one knows who did this or why.

▲ The *Mona Lisa* now hangs in the Louvre museum in Paris.

IT'S A FACT

Look closely at her smile. What does Mona Lisa know that we don't? For many years, mystery has surrounded da Vinci's work. People still debate Mona Lisa's true identity. Some people insist it is da Vinci himself. Others believe the painting is of several women combined into one.

Leonardo da Vinci used perspective to create the landscape. Trees and other objects shrink in size as they fade into the distance. The artist presents his subject in a pyramid-like **composition** (kahm-puh-ZIH-shuhn). Her crossed hands form the front corner of this pyramid. This structure helps to create depth. He used it in many of his other works as well.

Another important feature is the way da Vinci used color and shading. There are sharp contrasts of dark and light. For many, this creates a feeling of peace. In addition, he used lighter colors to paint Mona Lisa's face, neck, chest, and hands. This casts a gentle glow on his subject.

▲ This drawing is a perspective study for *Adoration of the Magi*, an unfinished work by Leonardo da Vinci.

Painters of the Renaissance

Michelangelo

Michelangelo was born Michelangelo Buonarroti. He's the only artist to rival Leonardo da Vinci for the title "Renaissance Man." Michelangelo was a sculptor, architect, painter, and writer. Like da Vinci, Michelangelo understood human anatomy and movement. He mastered **realism**. This is a way of painting something so that it looks like the real thing.

Michelangelo is most famous as the painter of the Sistine Chapel. He painted frescoes on the chapel's ceiling. To do this, he spent years lying flat on his back on platforms high above the floor.

▲ The Sistine Chapel shows nine scenes from Genesis. This book of the Bible tells of creation. The figures were originally painted without clothing. Their robes were added years later.

◄ At the center of the ceiling, Michelangelo painted the "birth of Adam."

Raphael

Raphael was born Raffaello Sanzio. He was deeply influenced by da Vinci's painting style.

In his short career, Raphael painted many great works of art. He is known for a group of **frescoes** in the pope's apartment in the Vatican. Raphael was a master of portrait painting. He showed the real emotions of his subjects. The realism helped make his work outstanding.

▲ Raphael painted *Madonna of the Goldfinch* in 1506. The work was done with oil paints on wood. Raphael's work shows linear perspective and the use of light and shade to create depth.

◀ Raphael created several self-portraits, including this painting.

RENAISSANCE SCULPTURE

Before the Renaissance, sculpture was mainly used to decorate buildings. The Catholic Church commissioned most works for churches. Renaissance sculptors created some nonreligious works of art. These sculptures were like those in ancient Greece and Rome. Sculptors used realism to create the figures.

Early Sculptors of the Renaissance

Italian artist Lorenzo Ghiberti (jih-BAYR-tee) was a leader in Renaissance sculpture. His sculpted figures showed emotions. He also used dramatic poses. His work influenced other Renaissance sculptors.

Ghiberti's most famous work was two sets of bronze doors. He created the doors for the Florence Baptistery. The doors included twenty-eight panels featuring religious subjects.

Ghiberti began a sculpting workshop after he received this commission. It took him and his students twenty years to complete the doors. One of his assistants was Donatello. Donatello later became the greatest sculptor of the early Renaissance.

✔ POINT

MAKE
CONNECTIONS

Compare a sculpture pictured in this book with one you've seen in your own home, school, or community. How are they alike? How are they different?

▲ Twenty-three of the bronze door panels by Ghiberti showed the life of Jesus Christ.

HISTORICAL PERSPECTIVE

The types of sculpting tools and mediums have greatly increased over time. Some Renaissance sculpture was done in wood or clay. Many pieces, however, were carved from stone or marble. Artists used simple tools like hammers and chisels. Today, most sculptors use soft materials like clay. Most **modeling** is done by hand. Modeling is the forming of a sculpture. Artists then use hand tools to carve details or trim away the clay.

Donatello

Many people consider Donatello to be the greatest sculptor of all time. His early works inspired other Renaissance sculptors.

Donatello came from Florence, but he spent a few years living in Rome. He studied art from the Roman Empire. His work reflects his study of classical style.

In his career, Donatello worked with many techniques and materials. He **cast** bronze sculptures. This means an artist creates a mold of the sculpture. He was the first sculptor to use perspective. He also developed **schiacciato** (SKEE-ah-chee-AH-toh). Works done in this style look as if they have depth. But they are actually formed on a shallow, flat surface.

◀ Donatello shows David unclothed. This was almost never done in the Middle Ages. Soon, other sculptors began to sculpt nude figures. This was a classical way of celebrating the human body.

Donatello's skill helped him sculpt his subjects with **realism**. He revealed the human form at its most self-confident.

▲ Donatello completed *St. Mark* in 1413 while still in his mid-twenties. The work is like the portrait sculptures of the Roman era.

CAREERS

ART RESTORER

An art restorer recreates the original appearance of an artwork. This career requires a special education. People study art in college. They learn how to repair and clean paintings. They clean small sections using cotton swabs. Trained art restorers fill in missing paint. Art restorers also use computers to do their work. Computers helped art restorers repair the Sistine Chapel. This job took twenty years to complete. One computer program diagramed every damaged section of the fresco.

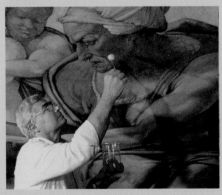

▲ This photo shows chemical solutions being used to clean a section of the ceiling of the Sistine Chapel.

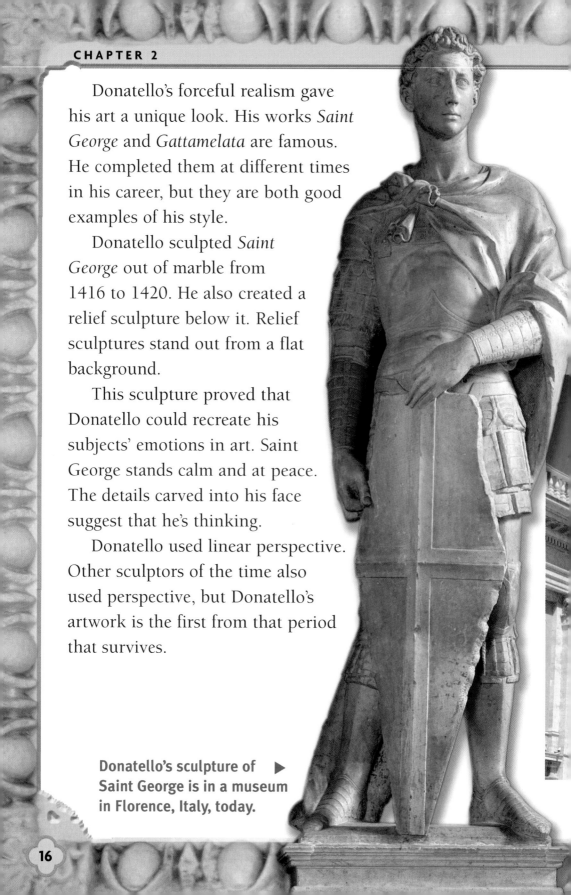

Donatello's forceful realism gave his art a unique look. His works *Saint George* and *Gattamelata* are famous. He completed them at different times in his career, but they are both good examples of his style.

Donatello sculpted *Saint George* out of marble from 1416 to 1420. He also created a relief sculpture below it. Relief sculptures stand out from a flat background.

This sculpture proved that Donatello could recreate his subjects' emotions in art. Saint George stands calm and at peace. The details carved into his face suggest that he's thinking.

Donatello used linear perspective. Other sculptors of the time also used perspective, but Donatello's artwork is the first from that period that survives.

Donatello's sculpture of ▶ **Saint George is in a museum in Florence, Italy, today.**

Between 1447 and 1453, Donatello created a bronze statue of Italian general Gattamelata. He is pictured in action riding his horse. The **equestrian** (ih-KWES-tree-uhn) statue stands more than 11 feet (3.3 meters) high. Many think that *Gattamelata* is one of the most symmetrical sculptures ever created. Symmetrical means that there is a balanced arrangement of parts. The balance can be on either side of a line or around a central point.

Over time, Donatello's style of modeling became even more exact. Other sculptors copied his style and techniques.

▲ Today, Donatello's *Gattamelata* stands in Padua, Italy.

CASTING

Sculptors often cast their work in metal or other substances. First, the artist creates a mold of the piece. Then the sculptor pours melted metal, cement, or even plastic into the mold. The piece is left to harden.

The sculptor takes away the mold. This leaves an exact copy of the original. Today, sculptors have electric tools. Artists use grinders to reshape small sections of the work. They use welders to cut and shape pieces, and to join pieces together.

Sculptors of the Renaissance

Michelangelo

Michelangelo is one of the greatest sculptors of all time. As a teenager, he studied sculpture in Florence. He attended the famous sculpture school in the Medici (MEH-dee-chee) gardens. Then, he went to Rome to study ancient ruins.

While there, Michelangelo carved one of the world's best-known sculptures. The *Pietá* (pee-ay-TAH) shows Mary holding her dead son, Jesus. Most sculpture of the time included decorative elements, but Michelangelo's work was simpler. As a result, his larger-than-life figures appear more forceful. Michelangelo's *Pietá* helped start his career.

▲ Michelangelo believed that hi role as a sculptor was to unco the figure that existed beneat the stone. One of his greatest works, *David*, is at the Academ in Florence, Italy. The marble figure is more than 14 feet (4. meters) tall.

◀ Today, the *Pietá* stands in St. Peter's Basilica in Rome.

Benvenuto Cellini

Benvenuto Cellini (cheh-LEE-nee) was famous in Florence in the 1500s. He was a sculptor and engraver. His favorite medium was metal, especially gold and silver.

Cellini had many powerful patrons, including the pope. Leaders of the day hired him to create coins. He put pictures of his patrons on the coins. He also created medallions, or necklaces, for patrons.

The gods of ancient Rome were some of Cellini's favorite subjects. He sculpted large silver statues of Jupiter, Vulcan, and Mars. One of his best-known works pictured figures from a Roman myth. It was a bronze statue of Perseus holding the head of Medusa.

▲ Cellini made this sculpture out of gold, enamel, and ivory for the king of France. One figure represents Earth. The temple next to Earth was meant to store peppercorns. The other figure stands for the sea. The boat beside him was for holding salt.

RENAISSANCE ARCHITECTURE

Column 20 Modules or 10 Diameters

Architecture also changed during the Renaissance. In the 1400s, architects in Italy borrowed elements from ancient Greece and Rome for their designs.

These included **vaults**, domes, columns, and arches. Architecture with these Greek and Roman features is described as classical.

▲ Renaissance architects were inspired by the ruins of ancient Greece and Rome. The Acropolis in Athens, Greece, is a ruin from the classical period.

Architecture in Italy

Architecture was very important in Renaissance Italy. Architects designed many churches, chapels, and other religious buildings. Over time, wealthy patrons influenced architecture. Powerful families financed the design and building of nonreligious buildings. Some hired architects to construct palaces. Others had civic buildings designed. Civic means for public use.

▼ The Coliseum in Rome is a lasting tribute to the architects of ancient Rome.

CLASSICAL FEATURES

vault

arch

dome

column

Eyewitness Account

"The Florentines excel other nations in all they apply themselves to. Apart from commerce, which is the real foundation of their city, they are reputed to be great men and skillful; expert also in the arts of painting, sculpture, architecture, which they exercise at home and abroad. It was they who revived the study of Greek and Latin. I have always been very much surprised to see that in these men . . . there should dwell so great a spirit and such high and noble thoughts."

—Florentine historian Benedetto Varchi (1503–1565)

Entablature 5 Mod

Column 20 Modules or 10 Diameters

Entablature's Mod

Column 20 Modules or 10 Diameters

Filippo Brunelleschi

Filippo Brunelleschi (broo-nah-LESS-kee) created the Renaissance style of architecture. He first trained as a goldsmith. Then he became interested in architecture and math. Brunelleschi went with his friend Donatello to Rome. There, the architect studied ancient Roman ruins.

Brunelleschi began a new style of building. His designs borrowed features from ancient Greece and Rome. He designed the churches of Santo Spirito and San Lorenzo in Florence. They are both examples of his classical style.

Brunelleschi experimented with weights, wheels, clocks, and gears. These early experiments led to new inventions. He created a hoisting, or lifting, device. The hoist enabled him to complete his most famous work. This was the dome over the Cathedral of Florence.

▲ The arches and columns in Brunelleschi's San Lorenzo are two classical features.

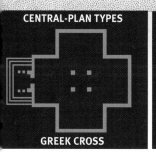

CENTRAL-PLAN TYPES

GREEK CROSS

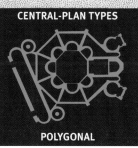

CENTRAL-PLAN TYPES

POLYGONAL

◀ Many religious buildings from the Renaissance had a central structure. The Greek-cross style was popular. The polygonal, or many-sided, style was popular, too.

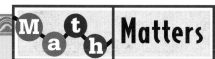

Math Matters

Filippo Brunelleschi developed technology that changed architecture. He invented hoists. The hoists used a system of counterweights and wheels. These made it possible to lift heavy building materials. With his invention, one pair of oxen could lift loads that once took six pairs of oxen to lift.

Column 20 Modules or 10 Diameters

In 1418, church officials held a design contest for the dome. It was to be the crowning glory of the cathedral. Someone had to figure out a way to build it. Many believed it was impossible to build such a large dome so high off the ground. The dome would rest on an eight-sided part of the cathedral. This was an additional challenge.

Brunelleschi's Dome

Many artists competed to win the dome contest. Prize money and fame were at stake. Brunelleschi began his plan for the dome. The Medici family supported his work. The contest caused a rivalry between Brunelleschi and the sculptor Ghiberti.

Brunelleschi's design was chosen after much debate and disagreement. His plan was unlike anything ever done before. He designed a double self-supporting shell. A rib structure also helped to support the dome's heavy load. Amazingly, the dome would be built without using a frame. This had never been done before.

✔ POINT
READ MORE ABOUT IT
To learn more about architecture long ago and today, visit the library and architecture sites on the Internet.

▲ Today, Brunelleschi's Dome still crowns the Cathedral of Florence.

Brunelleschi chose brick as the building material. He designed it in a spiral pattern. His design required new construction methods. These included his hoist.

In 1423, he was put in charge of the project. It continued for the rest of his life. The completion of the dome came in stages. By 1434, the main structure was completed. The project was finished in 1461. The last step was placing a lantern on top of the dome. Sadly, Brunelleschi didn't see the event. The architect died in 1446.

HISTORICAL PERSPECTIVE

Look above you. Is there anything special about the ceiling? Is there a work of art painted on it? Does it contain interesting features such as arches? The answer to all three questions is probably "no." Your answer might be different if you had lived during the Renaissance.

Ceilings in Renaissance buildings were important to any design. If you lived in a Renaissance villa, or large country estate, the ceilings might look like one of the three shown below.

vaulted ceiling

coffered ceiling

ceiling with works of art

Architects of the Renaissance

Leon Battista Alberti

Many people think Leon Battista (bah-TEES-tah) Alberti (al-BEAR-tee) is the greatest architect of all time. Besides architecture, he studied mathematics, philosophy, law, art, and music.

Alberti worked with other architects on some buildings. He completed only a few designs by himself. These included the churches San Sebastiano and San Andrea.

To design San Andrea, Alberti used many features from ancient Rome. Some say San Andrea is similar to the Pantheon in Rome.

Column 20 Modules or 10 Diameters

The Palazzo Rucellai was one ▶ of the few buildings designed by Leon Battista Alberti. The building had three floors. It used all three kinds of classical columns—Doric, Ionic, and Corinthian.

Andreas Palladio

Andreas Palladio (pah-LAY-dee-oh) was another Renaissance architect who copied the styles of ancient Rome. In fact, Palladio followed the writings of Vitruvius. He was a famous Roman architect.

Palladio is mostly remembered for his villas. He often used a classical front. The front looked like a temple, complete with columns.

> ### IN THEIR OWN WORDS
> *"Was anything unknown to him? He excels with ease and rapidity."*
> —The poet Poliziano referring to Leon Battista Alberti

▲ The Rotonda, or "Villa Capra," designed by Andreas Palladio is in Vicenza, Italy.

CONCLUSION

New ideas and discoveries during the Renaissance changed art forever. Art expanded to include more than just religious subjects. Painters began creating landscapes. They drew scenes of daily life. Portraits of nonreligious people were also popular.

Techniques of painting were transformed during the Renaissance. Great painters, such as Leonardo da Vinci, mastered new techniques of perspective. They created three-dimensional masterpieces. Painters and sculptors used realism to show the human form and emotions. Many Renaissance techniques and styles are still used today.

about 1430

Donatello completes his sculpture of David. Some art scholars consider it the first true example of Renaissance sculpture.

1504

Michelangelo completes his marble statue of David.

Leonardo da Vinci completes the *Mona Lisa.*

1506

▲ Monticello was the home of Thomas Jefferson, the third president of the United States. The design shows the influence of the Renaissance architect Andreas Palladio.

1508-1512

Michelangelo paints frescoes on the ceiling of the Sistine Chapel.

Rome is invaded by forces of Charles V, emperor of the Holy Roman Empire. Renaissance artists flee the city. Some consider this to be the official end of the Renaissance.

1527

Around the world, painters rely on perspective. It helps them create realism in their art. The details of anatomy introduced by Leonardo da Vinci are still admired.

Renaissance art still inspires artists. In museums, art students gather around Renaissance masterpieces. They try to understand the brilliance displayed so many centuries ago.

▼ St. Peter's Basilica

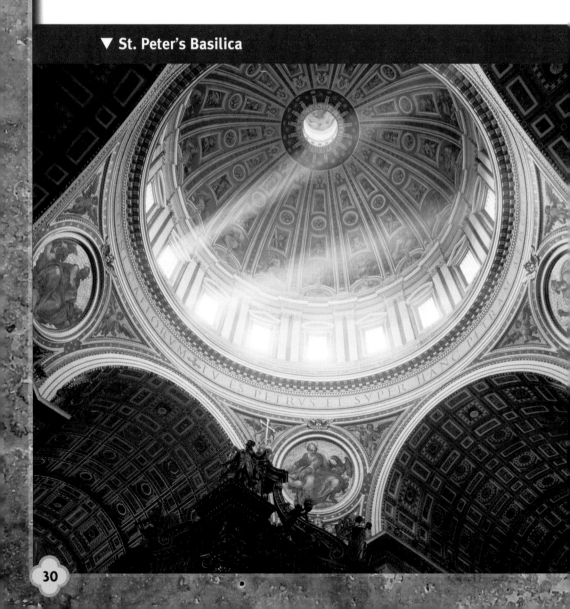

GLOSSARY

architecture (AHR-kih-tehk-chuhr) the creative process and physics of designing and building structures (page 3)

cast (KAST) the process of creating a sculpture by pouring a melted substance such as a metal into a mold (page 14)

commission (kuh-MIH-shuhn) money paid to a person, such as an artist, to perform a task or create a work of art (page 6)

composition (kahm-puh-ZIH-shuhn) the way in which two or more things are arranged (page 9)

equestrian (ih-KWEHS-tree-uhn) having to do with a figure on horseback (page 17)

fresco (FREHS-koh) a painting created by brushing watercolors on a layer of damp plaster spread on a wall or ceiling (page 11)

humanist (HYOO-mah-nihst) someone who believes in the study of the art and philosophies of ancient Greece and Rome (page 3)

modeling (MAH-duh-lihng) the forming of a work of sculpture by hand (page 13)

patron (PAY-truhn) one who financially supports the creation of art or literature (page 4)

perspective (puhr-SPEHK-tihv) a law of nature whereby the size of an object decreases as its distance from the eye increases (page 5)

realism (REE-uh-lih-zuhm) the representation in art of the natural world without idealization or distortion (page 10)

schiacciato (SKEE-ah-chee-AH-toh) a sculpting approach in which a work done on a shallow flat surface is made to look as if it has depth (page 14)

vault (VAHLT) an arched ceiling made of brick, stone, wood, or plaster (page 20)

INDEX